When Time Is at a Premium

By the same author

Attitudes in Rational Emotive Behaviour Therapy (REBT):
Components, Characteristics and Adversity-related
Consequences

When Time Is at a Premium

*Cognitive-Behavioural Approaches to
Single-Session Therapy
and Very Brief Coaching*

Windy Dryden, Ph.D

Rationality Publications

Rationality Publications
136 Montagu Mansions, London W1U 6LQ
www.rationalitypublications.com
info@rationalitypublications.com

First edition published by Rationality Publications
Copyright (c) 2016 Windy Dryden

A catalogue record of this book is
available from the British Library.

First edition 2016

ISBN: 978-1-910301-35-7

Printed and bound in Great Britain by
Lightning Source UK Ltd,
Chapter House, Pitfield, Kiln Farm,
Milton Keynes MK11 3LW

Contents

Preface

Cognitive-behavioural approaches to both therapy and coaching are normally designed to be brief interventions, although they can, of course be applied to longer term therapy and ongoing coaching. In this book, I show how it is to possible to work very briefly with people in both a therapy and a coaching context. In these times of increasing need and limited resources, it is my view that therapists and coaches need to be flexible and be able to offer a range of services to a varied clientele. As the title of this book indicates, sometimes, for a variety of reasons, time is a premium and therapists and coaches are called upon to work very briefly with people. If they wish to rise to this challenge, particularly if they already have a background in cognitive-behavioural interventions, then they may find this book of value.

First, a word about therapy and coaching. Most people in both disciplines would probably agree that the main task of therapy is to address emotional problems, while the main task of coaching is to help people, who are not struggling with emotional problems, to get more out of themselves, their work and their relationships. However, this distinction is not as clear-cut in practice as it is in theory and there are times in therapy when the therapist is called upon to help clients with objectives that are more developmental in nature. There are also certainly times in coaching when coaches are called upon to help coachees address their disturbed responses regarding adversities that may occur as a direct result of pursuing development-based objectives or in the course of daily living and unconnected with the coaching enterprise.

Thus the compleat therapist and coach needs to acquire and hone a varied range of skills to address both issues of disturbance and growth or establish and grow a referral network where they can refer to practitioners who specialise in areas where they lack the skills to help. This book is relevant no matter which of the above two stances you may adopt.

Next a word about language. In this book I refer to the consumers of therapy as 'clients' and to the consumers of coaching as 'coachees'. I am aware that many do not care for the term 'coachee', but I personally like it and it helps me as writer and you as reader to distinguish between issues more properly regarded as falling within the purview of therapy and issues more properly regarded as falling within the purview of coaching.

This book is divided into two parts. In Part 1, I describe a form of single-session therapy that I have developed which I call 'Single-Session Integrated Cognitive Behaviour Therapy' (SSI-CBT), which is a four points of contact model that falls within the definition of Single-Session Therapy developed by Moshe Talmon (1990), one of the pioneers in this field. In Part 2, I describe a form of very brief coaching that I have also developed and which I call 'Very Brief Cognitive Behavioural Coaching' (VBCBC), which can range between one and three sessions.

I will assume that you have some prior knowledge of cognitive-behavioural approaches to therapy and coaching, but if not I suggest the following texts to bring you up to speed:

- Dryden, W. (ed.) (2012) *Cognitive Behaviour Therapies*. London: Sage.

- Neenan, M. and Palmer, S. (eds) (2012) *Cognitive-behavioural Coaching in Practice: An Evidence Based Approach*. Hove, East Sussex: Routledge.

While there are, of course, areas of overlap between SSI-CBT and VBCBC, I will treat them separately in this book as I am aware that some readers will only be interested in one approach and not the other. I hope readers who are interested in both areas will pardon the repetition of some ideas in both parts of the book. I also invite all readers to give me feedback on the book by emailing me at windy@windydryden.com or at info@rationalitypublications.com

Windy Dryden
July 2016
London & Eastbourne

*This book is dedicated to the pioneering work of
Moshe Talmon and Michael Hoyt
in the field of single-session therapy*

PART 1

SINGLE-SESSION INTEGRATED COGNITIVE BEHAVIOUR THERAPY (SSI-CBT)

Overview

In this first part of the book, I describe an approach to therapy that I have devised entitled 'Single Session Integrated Cognitive-Behaviour Therapy' (SSI-CBT). I discuss the nature of this approach, its indications and contraindications, helpful therapist and client characteristics that are associated with a good outcome, what good practice is in SSI-CBT. Then, I discuss issues that occur at each of the four points of contact of SSI-CBT.

1

What Is Single-Session Integrated Cognitive Behaviour Therapy (SSI-CBT)?

1.1   Introduction

The subject of single-session therapy is quite controversial, because some think that there is very little that can be done in a single session. Others in the field, particularly those in private practice, are concerned about how they are going to earn a living if they only see somebody for one session of therapy.

While I will consider these and other related issues in this book, my priority is to outline a four-contact model of single-session therapy from a CBT perspective that I have developed, called 'Single-Session Integrated Cognitive Behaviour Therapy' or SSI-CBT (Dryden, 2017). These four points of contact are: (i) the very first contact; (ii) the pre-session telephone call; (iii) the face-to-face session; and (iv) the follow-up session. In this chapter, I will highlight two aspects of the approach which are distinctive features: (1) the importance of helping clients deal with adversity and (2) the importance of preparing adequately for the work by drawing upon a range of client variables that may facilitate the process of SSI-CBT.

1.2   What is SSI-CBT?

SSI-CBT is a perspective on single-session work that is broadly CBT in its foundations and makes use of insights from the three major 'waves' identified by Steven Hayes (2004). Thus, it is open to the insights from non-cognitive behaviour therapy (Wave 1), from cognitive modification based therapy (Wave 2) and a mindfulness acceptance type of approach (Wave 3). It is possible to utilise any and all of these particular approaches within the SSI-CBT framework (see Dryden, 2012).

My particular approach to single-session work, which I call SSI-CBT (WD), indicates that I am influenced by a number of people in the field and that the approach that is integrated. Let me highlight some of these influences before I outline the general approach itself.

The primary influence on my work was a book written by an Israeli therapist, Moshe Talmon (1990), who has been particularly instrumental in developing the field of single-session therapy. In addition, I incorporate some, but not all, of the ideas that emanate from the solution-focused approach. I particularly value this approach's emphasis on solutions, but don't agree with the position that it takes on 'problems' (Ratner, George and Iveson, 2012). Thus, here, I take the pluralistic position of dealing with problems and goals rather than just dealing with solutions. I also draw upon Scott Kellogg's (2015) transformational chair work in order to increase the emotional impact of my approach and draw on and make use of the work that has been done on using clients' strengths in therapy (Jones-Smith, 2014).

In addition, from a CBT perspective, SSI-CBT:

- recognises the importance of behaviour and of putting learning into practice as quickly as possible;

- focuses on the impact of a variety of cognitions – inferences, beliefs, schemas – expressed in a number of ways: words and images, at different levels of awareness;

- stresses, as noted above, the importance of making, if possible, an emotional impact in the time that therapists have with their clients; and

- prioritises the importance of clients taking away new meaning, in a form that is memorable to them and that they can use in appropriate situations.

However, I want to stress that, as I conceive it, there is not a single approach to single-session CBT work. Rather, it is best seen as a framework and what I want to do in Part 1 of this book is to outline this framework. Having said that while my position is that SSI-CBT can be applied by therapists who practise different approaches within the CBT, my own practice of SSI-CBT, which I call SSI-CBT (WD), is influenced by the theory and practice of Rational Emotive Behaviour Therapy (REBT) as originated by Albert Ellis (1994).

When he was alive Ellis used to run what he called the Friday Night Workshop at the Albert Ellis Institute (AEI) where he interviewed two volunteers on their emotional problem. These sessions were, in effect, brief single sessions of REBT and they taught me the importance of creating and staying focused while helping the client to do the same. They also taught me the importance of helping clients to use the limited time available to deal with rather than bypass adversity.

1.3   The Importance of Dealing with Adversity in SSI-CBT

It is my view that in all forms of CBT, whether the therapeutic work is ongoing, short-term, very short-term or single-session, it is important for therapists to help their clients to deal with the adversities they actually face or think they face. If not, clients will keep struggling to deal with these adversities in actuality and/or in their minds.

Thus, if you, as therapist, are helping a client to deal with public-speaking anxiety where he (in this case) is anxious about his mind going blank, then, in my view it is crucial to help him to face the prospect that his mind could go blank so that you can encourage him to deal effectively with this eventuality, rather than help him, for example, to prepare for the speech so thoroughly that in his view it is highly unlikely that his mind will go blank.

Generally, if you do not help people to deal with an adversity, such as their mind going blank, they will become stuck and be unable to move on from the troublesome negative emotion that they experience about the adversity. Thus, one of the main goals of SSI-CBT, as I envisage it, is to help people to become unstuck and to move on, so that they can continue a process, which you, as therapist, can help them to take forward.

1.4   Drawing on a Range of Client Variables

As I will discuss more fully later, it is important, when you are doing single-session work, to prepare thoroughly for the process and this involves identifying a range of client variables upon which you can draw as necessary during that process. Some of these client variables include:

- the strengths that clients have that they can access during the SSI-CBT process;

- the people who have been the most helpful to clients over the years and what they did that was helpful so that you may be able to replicate the ingredients of that help;

- memorable occasions of being helped and what was 'helpful' about these episodes, again to help you use such helpful ingredients in SSI-CBT;

- healthy principles that clients have used over the years that you can encourage them to use;
    ⇒ For example, my mother used to say to me, 'Son, if you don't ask, you don't get!' I modified this principle thus, 'Yes, if you don't ask, you don't get, but asking does not guarantee you getting.'

- clients' healthy role models: once you have identified who these are and why they are role models for your clients, you can refer to these people and what they stand for during the process;

- clients' preferred learning styles: once identified you can utilise this information at important junctures during the process.

2

Who Can Benefit from SSI-CBT?

My view is that many clients could potentially benefit from SSI-CBT and I will answer this question by grouping such people under a number of different headings.

2.1 People with Non-clinical Problems

For many years I have given brief demonstrations of my CBT-based work with a volunteer who is seeking help with a current and genuine problem. These sessions take place in front of an audience of people working in the field of mental health in some capacity. My intention is to offer some help to the volunteer within the constraints of a short demonstration (about 20 minutes in length). For which problems or issues do the volunteers seek help? An informal analysis shows that the most common issues are in frequency order: anxiety, procrastination, a range of emotional problems (such as guilt, shame, hurt, jealousy, envy), self-esteem issues, uncertainty, anger, lack of control, problems in relationships, life dilemmas and quandaries, and decision-making.

While these problems may not be seen as 'clinical'[1] in nature, they are troubling for the individual and, if not dealt with, may lead to problems more clinical in nature.

---

[1] The distinction between problems that are 'clinical' and 'non-clinical' in nature is often not an easy one to make. However, here, by a 'non-clinical' problem I mean a problem that has a negative impact on the person's life but less so than if the problem was 'clinical' and where the

In Britain, it is difficult to get professional help for problems which would not be considered 'clinical' in nature and thus there is a need for a service that could provide help for people with problems such as those outlined above. SSI-CBT therapists could well provide such a service. This is particularly the case if the person seeking help is 'ready to take care of business' or 'ready to go'. I use such phrases simply because these are phrases used by people seeking immediate and brief help for their problems. If you are 'ready to go', you don't want to be told by your doctor that your problems are not severe enough to warrant a referral or if you are offered help on the National Health Service, you do not want to be told that you will be put on a waiting list, but will have to wait a long time because people with more severe problems will have greater priority. You want to take advantage of the moment and this is what SSI-CBT is designed to help you do.

The goal of SSI-CBT here is to help people with non-clinical problems who have become 'stuck' with these problems to become unstuck and move on in a short period of time; not necessarily 'cured', but able to be helped to initiate a process and carry on this process on their own.

2.2 People Who View Therapy as Intermittent Help through the Life Cycle

Some people consider therapy like going to the doctor. Thus, if they have a problem they may seek help briefly, but once they get help they stop going. Later, if they have another problem they may return for more brief help and continue in

---

symptoms are less intense and troubling to the person than it would be if it was a 'clinical' problem.

this way across the life cycle. A lot of people therefore do not share the views of practitioners that therapy is an ongoing process. They see it as something they can pick up and use when they need to. SSI-CBT fits with the expectations of such people.

2.3 People Who Require Prompt and Focused Crisis Management

Such people are in crisis, they hurt, but they tend to be ready for and keen to initiate change. If you can rise to this challenge, then you can help such people quite quickly, often in a single session.

2.4 People with Clinical Problems Who Want Help with Non-clinical Problems

While SSI-CBT has not been designed to help people with clinical problems, particularly when these are severe, it is the case that such people may also have non-clinical problems. Thus, people with borderline personality disorder may also need help, in the short term, to overcome their anxiety about giving a talk in order to get a job. Just because somebody has got a particular diagnosis does not mean, in my view, that you cannot help the person with their non-clinical problem so long as the therapeutic contract is clear.

2.5 People Who Have Clinical Problems

As I have just stated, SSI-CBT has not been designed for people with clinical problems. However, there are a number of examples of single-session CBT work that have been designed to help people address such problems. Thus, Lars Öst developed an extended single-session CBT-based therapy for the treatment for specific phobias (see Zlomke and Davis, 2008).[2] This approach combines exposure, participant modelling, cognitive challenges and reinforcement. Reinecke (e.g. Reinecke, Waldenmaier, Cooper and Harmer, 2013) has developed an experiential-based single-session treatment for panic disorder which combines psychoeducation of a leading CBT conceptualisation of panic and its treatment with an immediate opportunity to practise this treatment in a confined space where people would normally experience panic. Having said that CBT has been modified to help people with clinical problems within a single-session format, it is important to emphasise that clients who seem to benefit from these approaches are those who:

- understand what the treatment involves and what they are expected to do and agree to go forward based on this understanding;

- are prepared to take care of business quickly; and

- are prepared to tolerate quite a bit of discomfort to achieve their goals.

---

[2] Whether by chance or design, Öst called his approach 'One Session Treatment', with the first letter of each word spelling out the name of the originator!

2.6   Drop-in or Walk-in Centres

Single-session work is very popular in countries where drop-in or walk-in services are common (e.g. Australia and Canada). In Britain, drop-in centres have been set up for people who are quite chaotic in their lives (e.g. they may have drink problems or addiction problems). Such people, in general, will not make an appointment to see a therapist or, if they do, they tend not to keep it, no matter how many times they may receive text reminders. Indeed, they may not even have a phone. If you work in a drop-in centre, it is important to assume that you will only see the person once and plan the therapeutic work accordingly.

2.7   Coaching

In my experience, a single-session framework works well in coaching. Coaching is a way of working with people who seek to get more out of themselves, their work, their relationships and their lives in general. Such people are generally doing OK in their lives, but want more out of their lives, and have a sense that they are not fulfilling their potential. Although coaching is more of an ongoing process, or can be, it can also be used within a single-session format. This is particularly the case when somebody wants to kick-start a process, and then implement this process on their own. Such people tend to be autonomous in their approach to helping themselves and come to coaching to gain a sense of direction. When they have that direction they want to pursue it by themselves. In another case these people may have a single development-based objective with which they want help, and they only come for single-session coaching to discover the best way for them to achieve this objective. Once they have done so again they wish to implement their learning by themselves.

In addition to helping people identify development-based objectives and the best way to achieve them, my own experience of helping people within the single-session coaching framework has been to assist them to identify and deal with the obstacles that they encounter which impede them from working towards their development-based objectives. In such cases, the single-session coaching is obstacle- and adversity-focused.

I will discuss my approach to very brief cognitive behavioural coaching (VBCBC) in the second part of this book.

2.8   Psychoeducation

There are a group of people who are open to therapy, but want to try it first before committing themselves to the process. This is not unusual in other spheres of life. Thus, if you are considering a new toothpaste you will try a taster size tube first before committing yourself to a standard size tube. The same is true with skin care products. To those people who want to 'taste' therapy, in general or CBT, in particular before they commit themselves to it, then the SSI-CBT therapist would say, 'Let's try it. Commit yourself to one session, and let's see what I can do to help you. Let me show you how CBT could help you, if you have issues that will take a while to address.' In this case, you are offering a single session as a form of psychoeducation where you demonstrate how you would tackle an issue. In doing so, you may well help the person with their problem so that they need no further therapy. Or if not, they will have a clearer idea how you would address their issue.

2.9   Other Scenarios

In addition to the above SSI-CBT may be suitable for people in the following scenarios

2.9.1   Reluctant Clients

Some people are reluctant to go to therapy and will only commit themselves to one session. In this case as a therapist, what do you do? Will you turn them away or are you going to help them? Again the SSI-CBT therapist would offer the person what they are prepared to commit to and try and deal with their issue in that single session.

2.9.2   Therapy Trainees

In general therapy trainees need to be in therapy in the approach in which they are being trained. However, if they wish to experience other approaches that they learn about rather than just read about them, what can they do? My stance is that if non-CBT trainees wish to experience what it is like to be a client in CBT, I am happy to give them the experience as long as they are prepared to bring a genuine, current problem for which they would like to receive help and I will offer them a single session to achieve this.

2.9.3   Clients Who Are Already in Therapy

I am prepared to offer SSI-CBT to clients who are already in therapy with other therapists when these therapists know about it and consent to it and when these clients: (a) are seeking a second opinion; (b) have problems that their therapist cannot or will not help them with.

2.9.4   People from Out of Town

Sometimes people have requested to see me for a single session because they are from out of town and want to see me when they are in town for a very limited period. I am happy to offer SSI-CBT in this circumstance.

2.9.5   People Who Volunteer for Demonstration Sessions

Whenever, I give a lecture on a therapeutic issue, I offer members of the audience an opportunity to volunteer for a brief single session of CBT in front of the audience. I have been doing this for many years and it follows in the tradition of Albert Ellis who used to run a Friday Night Workshop at the Albert Ellis Institute where he would interview two volunteers who would bring problems similar to those listed in the section above on 'people with non-clinical problems' (Ellis and Joffe, 2002). In addition, clients who volunteer for a videotaped demonstration session are volunteering for single-session therapy. This tradition goes back to the 'Gloria' trilogy of films where Gloria saw Carl Rogers, Fritz Perls and Albert Ellis for a single session of Client-Centred Therapy,[3] Gestalt Therapy and Rational-Emotive Therapy[4] respectively.

---

[3] Now known as Person Centred Therapy.
[4] Now known as Rational Emotive Behaviour Therapy.

3

Contraindications for SSI-CBT

While there are some in the single-session field who say, 'Single-session therapy can be helpful for everybody', I take the position that for SSI-CBT there are contraindications. Thus in my view SSI-CBT, in general, is not indicated for the following.

3.1 Clients Who Find it Hard to Connect With or Trust a Therapist

By its nature, SSI-CBT requires clients to be able to connect quickly with the therapist and engage immediately with their problems. This requirement rules out a number of clients who would struggle to do this. While most of these will not opt for SSI-CBT, the minority who do will usually indicate their ambivalence quite early and should be encouraged to seek a longer form of treatment.

3.2 Clients Who Don't Want CBT of Any Description

While the ideas of CBT appeal to many clients there are some who do not resonate with its ideas and practices and some who are outspoken in their hostility to this approach. For example, I once directed a CBT-based group therapy programme in a private UK hospital where patients began in supportive group therapy to settle them and then were transferred to CBT group therapy for a focused approach to their problem. While most people were keen to join the CBT programme, a minority wanted to remain in supportive group therapy against the advice of their psychiatrists. One exclaimed that he would kill himself if he was made to go into CBT. Clearly, it is not wise to foist CBT onto anyone and thus, SSI-CBT is not indicated for anyone who clearly does not want it!

3.3 Clients Who Require Ongoing Therapy for a Variety of Reasons

A number of people may want single-session therapy, but their problems are more chronic and complicated than can be helped within a single-session framework. Thus, they may have several problems with no linking themes, and their goals are quite ambitious and beyond the scope of single-session work.

3.4 Clients Who Are Quite Vague in Their Presentations

SSI-CBT requires clients to able to specify their problems and focus on one of them for the duration of the SSI-CBT process. There are some clients who are very vague in how they present their issues and cannot be specific even when encouraged to do so by the therapist. SSI-CBT is contraindicated for such people.

3.5   Clients Who Are Likely to Feel Abandoned by Their Therapist after the Single Session

There are some clients who can engage quickly with therapists, which as I pointed out above is a good sign for SSI-CBT, but would feel abandoned at the end of this process even though it is a very short one. As this would cause more problems than it would solve, SSI-CBT is not indicated for these clients.

Here, as elsewhere, it is important for therapists to be clear with clients who want SSI-CBT but are judged not to be suitable for it and to suggest alternative forms of treatment which are judged to be suitable. Such transparency normally is sufficient for clients to change their minds about wanting SSI-CBT, but when it doesn't my practice is to carry out SSI-CBT to see what happens. If I have been wrong in my initial I am delighted to have been proved so, but if I have been proved correct, at least the client has experiential evidence that SSI-CBT is not sufficient for their therapeutic needs and are usually willing to work with a more appropriate therapeutic format.

4

Helpful Client and Therapist Characteristics

There are certain client and therapist characteristics, which if present, increase the chances that SSI-CBT will be effective for clients. In this brief chapter, I will review both, beginning with helpful client characteristics for SSI-CBT.

4.1   Helpful Client Characteristics for SSI-CBT

If clients demonstrate the following characteristics, the prognosis is good for a favourable SSI-CBT outcome.

- They are ready to take care of business now.

- They are prepared to be as actively engaged in the process as they can.

- They can focus with clarity and specificity in articulating the main issue that they want to address and what they want to achieve from SSI-CBT.

- They are realistic about what can be achieved.

- They are prepared to put into practice what they learn from the process.

- They can move, or be helped to move, with relative ease, from the specific to the general and back again.

- They can relate to metaphors, aphorisms, stories and imagery.

- They are willing and able to engage in in-session activities such as chair work, role play and imagery.

- They have a sense of humour and can resonate to the therapist's sense of humour .

4.2   Helpful Therapist Characteristics for SSI-CBT

If therapists demonstrate the following characteristics, the prognosis is good for a favourable SSI-CBT outcome.

- They are realistic about what can be achieved from SSI-CBT.

- They can tolerate not having a lot of information about their clients.

- They think that they can help clients without first carrying out a full case formulation.

- They can quickly engage with clients.

- They can be what Arnold Lazarus (1993) called an 'authentic chameleon'. This means that therapists can change their way of relating to clients according to their ideas about what their clients need and to their clients' stated wishes.

- They can communicate clearly and succinctly with their clients.

- They are flexible and while they may have preferred strategies, they will use other strategies when their preferred ones do not seem to be helping their clients.

- They have a pluralistic outlook on the field, in general, and on single-session work in particular.

- They can think quickly on thier feet.

- They can move, with relative ease, from the specific to the general and back again and can facilitate such movement in their clients.

- They are good at devising bespoke metaphors, aphorisms, stories and appropriate imagery with their clients.

- They can elicit feedback from their clients and change their way of working on the basis of such feedback.

Of course if both sets of helpful therapist and client characteristics are present then this augurs very well for a positive client outcome from SSI-CBT.

5

Good Practice in SSI-CBT

In this chapter, I consider what is good practice in Single-Session Integrated CBT. Thus, it is good practice for SSI-CBT therapists to:

- Help clients to prepare for and to reflect on the work.

It is very important for clients to prepare for both the pre-session telephone call and for the face-to-face session and to give themselves time to reflect on both points of contact. It is thus good practice to suggest to clients that they turn off their mobile phones and tablets 30 minutes before these sessions so that they prepare themselves for them and to get themselves into a focused mindset and do the same after both sessions so that they can reflect on what they have learned.

Also to aid reflection, I record the face-to-face session, and provide clients with a copy of this and a written transcript of the session. These are included in the price of the SSI-CBT 'package'. I provide both since some people like to listen to the session that they have had with me, by going over the digital voice recording, while others people like to read about it. Both are ways of refreshing their memory of what we covered and indeed sometimes clients remark that listening to or reading the session highlighted an important point that they missed at the time. I should emphasise, however, that the use of recordings and transcripts are my own practice and are not an essential part of the SSI-CBT process.

- Engage clients quickly.

  In this respect, it is important to recognise that rapport is developed through the work. There is no rapport-building stage prior to getting down to doing the work of change.

- Be clear about what they can and what they cannot do within the session.

  Thus, while SSI-CBT therapists cannot address all their clients' problems, they can help their clients make a significant difference in one key area of their lives assuming that this issue is amenable to quick, focused intervention.

- Demonstrate a style that it is active-directive in nature, but to do so while encouraging their clients to be active, rather than rendered passive.

- Focus and keep their clients focused on the target problem.[5]

  In this way, productive work can be done. Leaving clients to wander all over the place while following them is to be avoided at all costs!

- Assess problems quickly.

- Work, if at all possible, with an imminent future example of their clients' target problem.

  Given that a major goal of SSI-CBT is to help the client deal with their target problem in the future, it is easier to do this if the focus is on a likely occurring future example of the problem than it is if a past example of the

---

[5] A target problem is the one issue that therapist and client have agreed to focus on in SSI-CBT.

problem is the focus of the work. Working with a future example of a target problem is facing forward all the time, while working with a past example is facing backwards and then turning around to face forwards to implement what has been learned from the past.

- Ensure that the work has a goal-orientated focus and, if possible, link that goal to a key client value.

  Then, it is good practice to remind clients of that value at relevant points in the process.

- Help clients understand that they will need to sacrifice something in order to achieve their goal.

  Helping clients get to the stage of being prepared to make this sacrifice is key to the success of the process.

- Be open and clear about what they are doing and why they are doing it, without being compulsive about doing so.

- Encourage their clients to be as specific as they can be, but to use opportunities for generalisation.

- Identify and make use of a variety of clients' strengths and resources described earlier in Part 1.

- Make liberal use of questions while ensuring that clients are given time to answer these questions.

- Listen carefully to the answers clients give to these questions and ask the question again if clients have not answered the question put to them and it is important that they do so.

- Check out clients' understanding of the main points that they wish to convey.

- Identify and deal with any doubts, reservations and objections that clients may have about any aspect of the SSI-CBT process, particularly those that clients express non-verbally.

- Have clients take away one key point that they can implement to make a real difference with respect to their target issue.

  There is a book called *The One Thing* (Keller and Papasan, 2012) which shows that, quite often, change happens in the business world if people can focus on, take away and apply one thing that they have learned from a conference, workshop or meeting. While SSI-CBT therapists may be tempted to give clients a lot to take away for future consideration, it is important that they do not act on that temptation. In SSI-CBT, 'less is more' and 'more is less'. If clients take away a lot of points they will generally end up confused and implement none of these points.

- Encourage clients to summarise the work done and to fill in missing points.

- Help clients to come up with a plan to implement what they have learned as soon as possible.

- Carry out a follow-up session so that the work can be evaluated.

- Offer clients more help if they need it. If clients ask for and are given more help, then the work cannot be regarded as SSI-CBT. However, it is important to remember that client welfare is more important than retaining the integrity of SSI-CBT, a point I will reiterate at the end of Part 1 of this book.

In the forthcoming chapters, I will provide an overview of the four points of contact that are featured in my model of Single-Session Integrated CBT. You may be wondering how SSI-CBT can be referred to as 'single-session' work if it has four points of contact. However, in my view, what still makes it single-session therapy is that it conforms to Moshe Talmon's (1990) definition. In his seminal book on SST, Talmon (1990: xv) says that 'Single-session therapy is defined here as one face-to-face meeting between a therapist and a patient with no previous or subsequent sessions within one year.' Telephone intake and follow-up are part of SST in that they are not face-to-face.

Here then are the four points of contact. In discussing them I will refer to my own practice and, in doing so, I want to stress that I am describing one person's practice of SSI-CBT and not *the* way of practising SSI-CBT. Thus, what I have to say should be regarded as *descriptive*, not *prescriptive*.

6

Contact 1: The Very First Contact

When somebody contacts me seeking my help, I outline the services that I offer. Here is an example of what I say:

- I offer *ongoing therapy* for people who have more complicated problems where we need some time to deal with them.

- I offer *brief time limited therapy* of up to 10 sessions for people whose problems can be dealt with in a reasonably short-period of time.

- I offer *single-session therapy* for people who have a single problem that can be dealt with in a very focused timely manner or who want advice on how to deal with a problem which they want to address on their own.

- I offer *ongoing coaching* for people who don't have any problems to deal with, but just a sense that they could get more out of their lives in a number of areas.

- I offer *very brief coaching* of between 1 and 3 sessions for people who don't have problems but who have a sense that they can get more out of their lives in one area or who want to kick-start a process that they want to continue on their own.

- I offer *couples therapy* for couples who have problems in their relationship. The length of this process depends on the nature of these problems and the commitment both partners have to address them.

Once I have described each service, I ask them to which service they are best suited. If they nominate single-session therapy, I will ask them to indicate, briefly, what they hope to achieve in that single session. If their answer is consistent with what SSI-CBT can offer, I will move to the next point of contact.

7

Contact 2: The Pre-Session Telephone Call

The next point of contact is a pre-session telephone call, which lasts about half an hour. I try to organise this a day or two after the initial contact. During this telephone call, my aim is twofold. First, I want to confirm or refute my initial sense that SSI-CBT is suitable for the person. If they are, my next goal is to ensure that we get the most out of the process. I do this by taking the person through a structured protocol which I present in Table 7.1.

Table 7.1   Pre-session telephone protocol

---

1. What made you decide that now is the right time for therapy?

2. How do you anticipate the issue could to be solved?

3. How soon do you think the issue could be solved?

4. How do you think I can best help you to deal with the issue?

5. What are the factors (or circumstances) that have contributed to the issue?

6. What have you tried to do that has helped with the issue?

7. What have you tried that has not helped with the issue?

8. What core values do you have that we might refer to in our work together in addressing your problem?

9. What strengths do you have as a person that you can use that might help you address the issue?

10. Can you tell me about an occasion where you made a significant change in outlook in a very short period of time?

11. Who do you consider to be a role model who might directly or indirectly be helpful to you as you deal with the problem?

12. I would like to know what your preferred way of learning is so that I can tailor the session to best help you. Can you help shed light on this?

13. Between now and our face-to face-session, I want you to notice the things that happen to you that you would like to keep happening in the future relevant to the problem. In this way, you will help me to find out more about your goal.

14. Is there anything that you would like me to know that will help me prepare for our face-to-face session or that would help us get the most out of the session?

I will use the information that I obtain in the face-to-face session, which is the next point of contact. My aim is to schedule this session within seven days of the pre-session telephone contact.

8

Contact 3: The Face-to-Face Session

My face-to-face sessions last up to 50 minutes although they may be longer if necessary.

8.1 Beginning the Face-to-Face Session

At the beginning of the face-to-face session, I generally ask for an update since the pre-session telephone contact. If the client has experienced a change then I ask what they did to bring about the change and then use this later to help them capitalise on the change. I found that occasionally a client would ring up to cancel the face-to-face session saying that they had solved the problem after the telephone session. This prompted me to rethink how I charge for the SSI-CBT package. I now explain that a percentage of the fee is due at the end of the telephone session and the remainder is due before the face-to-face session

If the client had agreed to do anything after the telephone session, I will check on this. Sometimes, I may send a client an email summary of what was covered in the telephone session, and, if so, I will ask if there are any matters arising from that summary.

8.2   Creating a Focus

At an early stage of the face-to-face session, it is very important to create a focus. What is a focus? It is a concentration on a clear and central point. The focus includes a problem, a solution or goal, and, in my view, in SSI-CBT it should cover both.

8.3   Maintaining the Focus

Once you have established a focus with your client it is important to keep to it, unless there is a good reason to change it. If you change it, you have had, what I call, a false start. When this happens, quickly negotiate a new start with the client. If the focus is correct, you still need to help the client to keep to it, as it is natural for people to go from topic to topic in a conversation.

In an ordinary conversation this would not be a problem, but if it is allowed to happen in SSI-CBT, it will compromise the work that you will wish to do. So it is important that you intervene to keep your client on track. This involves reminding them what their target problem and related goals are. It may also involve you interrupting the client. Therapists are not good, in general, at interrupting clients. We think that it is rude or that we are interrupting what we refer to as 'the client's process', which some of us tend to view in sacred terms!

On the first point, my view is that it is rude *not* to interrupt the client in SSI-CBT. You have contracted to do a focused piece of work and anything that interferes with this focus is to be avoided.

On the second point, it might be argued that 'the client's process' is what has got them into the trouble with their target problem in the first place, and if so, you will want to interrupt it. My view that interrupting the client is best done with tact and when the client is primed to expect it and has given permission for it to happen. Thus, it is my practice to say something to my clients along the following lines, 'Because our time is limited together and we are working to help you to achieve your nominated goal, it is my goal to keep us both on track. This may involve me interrupting you from time to time if we go off track. Do I have your permission to do that?'

The vast majority of clients assent to this, often remarking that it would be a relief if I were to interrupt them because they realise that they may easily change the subject, if allowed to do so unchecked. I also ask my clients how I can best interrupt them and use their suggestion if I need to do so to bring them back to the focus during the process. I have dwelt on the topic of interrupting clients here because in my experience therapists often have a problem doing so!

8.4 Understanding/Assessing the Target Problem

Once you have agreed a target problem and related goal, the next stage is to understand or assess the target problem. In doing so, it is important, if possible, to assess a specific example of the problem – preferably, as I mentioned above, as it may occur in the imminent future. Assessment involves discovering what the main feeling the person experiences, what behaviours or action tendencies are involved and what thinking goes along with these feelings and behaviours. This thinking is different from the thinking that helps create the problem in the first place.

I will discuss this latter type of thinking below in the section entitled 'Identifying the Central Mechanism'. Also, and most importantly, you need to understand the nature of the adversity your client finds problematic. For example, let's suppose that a client says that she (in this case) is anxious about public speaking; you need to understand what it is precisely that she is anxious about? Let's assume that it is 'my mind going blank'. In this case, you will want to keep the focus on that adversity. Within the SSI-CBT framework, if you can help this client deal effectively with her mind going blank then you have helped her significantly.

8.5   Setting a Goal

Once you have understood the affective, behavioural and cognitive aspects of the client's problem and you know the nature of the adversity that they find problematic, the next step is to help them to set goals with respect to that adversity. My own approach to goal-setting in the face of adversity is to help the client to experience a healthy negative emotion rather than to feel an unhealthy negative emotion. Thus, in our case example as the person is anxious about her mind going blank, I would want to help her to feel concerned, but not anxious about this happening, since to feel nothing is not appropriate and to feel good is not appropriate. Also, to feel less anxious is problematic since if anxiety is an unhealthy response to the adversity, to experience less of it is still problematic.

Another issue would occur if the client in our example were to respond to a goal-setting question by saying, 'I want to be competent and confident at public speaking.' This is fine, but, in order for me to help her to do that, I first need to help her deal with the adversity about which she is currently anxious. So, I say something like, 'Is it better for me to try to help you to be competent and confident about speaking in public when you are scared of your mind going blank, or shall I help you deal with that particular anxiety first?' Most clients can understand that their problem needs to be dealt with first. Here, as elsewhere in the process, if you give clients a reasonable rationale, then you can bring them on board with your strategy.

Please note, then, that in my approach to goal-setting in SSI-CBT, the adversity stays the same, but the emotion, behaviour and associated thinking changes. Thus, in our example, 'My mind going blank,' is present in both the problem and the goal, because I want to help the client to deal with the adversity. If I don't do this, then the client will still have a problem with the adversity and will return to it time and time again. This is why they get stuck.

8.6 Identifying the Central Mechanism

What I mean by the 'central mechanism' is the factor that, from your theoretical perspective, mainly accounts for the problem. Given that SSI-CBT is underpinned by CBT theory, it is probable that your hypothesised central mechanism involves problematic cognitions, however you define them, and the behaviours that help to maintain them. In my approach to CBT, which is Rational Emotive Behaviour Therapy, the central mechanism is rigid and extreme attitudes that lie at the base of clients' target problems and the behaviours that stem from them. Whichever approach to CBT you practise, the central mechanism needs to come to the fore, if possible. If your client does not accept the role of the central mechanism that you have put forward, then you need to look at other ways of helping them. If you are flexible and pluralistic in your approach, you can do this.

8.7   Intervening with the Central Mechanism

Once I have identified the central mechanism that largely accounts for the client's target problem, my next step is to intervene with this mechanism. This involves me helping the client to develop alternative flexible and non-extreme attitudes that could form the basis of their healthy response to the adversity that they find problematic. It also involves me helping them to nominate alternative constructive behaviours that are consistent with these more functional attitudes and if enacted will help to strengthen and maintain them. Other CBT practitioners will have their own ways of dealing with the identified central mechanism. This point once again shows the importance of viewing SSI-CBT as a framework within to practise rather than a prescription for practice.

8.8   Making an Emotional Impact

In order for the work on the central mechanism to be more than a theoretical exercise for clients, it is important that you strive to make the experience an emotionally impactful one for them. This involves doing one or more of the following:

- Listen carefully to the words your clients use and see if they have an emotional reaction to particular words and phrases. Then use such language at judicious points in the process so that the clients can resonate with their own emotionally laden language.

- Watch for their reaction to the language that you employ and see again if they display an affective response to your words and phrases. Again use such language to connect them to their emotions to enhance the impact of the session.

- Structure your interventions in ways in which clients have indicated that they have found helpful in the past, so that you can better help them in the present.

- Mobilise and utilise their strengths.

- Make use of information pertaining to their role models and why they look up to such people.

- Make use of their preferred learning style.

- Refer to their core values and meanings at various points in the session and, in particular, encourage your clients to see that they are more likely to pursue their therapeutic goal when this is underpinned by a core value or meaning than when it is not.

- Your use of humour may have an emotional impact on clients.

- Appropriate therapist self-disclosure can also be quite helpful in inspiring some clients and thus making an impact. Recently, a client came to SSI-CBT because he felt devastated about losing an important report which he had not backed up. He could see no way to rescue the situation. With his permission, I told him the following story.

Many years ago, I was writing a book entitled 'Overcoming Shame' on an old Amstrad NC-200 portable word processor. Once I had finished the book I transferred the chapters to a floppy disk and took great care in doing so. I then wiped the machine's internal memory clean since I had other writing to do and needed the space. When I came to open the floppy disk, to my dismay it was empty. It transpired that in spite of my careful efforts the files had not been saved. I responded to this discovery by losing emotional control. I was angry with myself, the world, Amstrad and went around kicking pieces of furniture in my living room. This tantrum, for that's what it was, lasted for 20 minutes when I stopped, exhausted, and considered the irony of my response when I, a therapist, was trained to help others deal with adversity in healthier ways. So, I sat down and did the following:

First, I accepted myself for my reaction – showing myself that being a psychologist did not render me immune from reacting very humanly, albeit in a self-defeating manner. Second, I accepted reality. Yes, it was very, very bad to lose the work as I did, but it had happened and it was hardly the end of the world. Third, I realised that I had a decision to make. I could give up on the book or start from scratch. I chose to do the later and two months later finished it. It was published later that year (Dryden, 1997).

My client resonated with my story, particularly the part about my initial reaction and how I responded to it. He used it to deal with his own emotional upset about his lost report and resolved to write it again starting when he got home. He emailed me a week later saying that he had finished it and received a positive response from his boss for his work. He attributed the success of SSI-CBT to my self-disclosure.

However, it is important to realise that not all clients react positively to therapist self-disclosure, so it is best to ask their permission to proceed before making the disclosure.

The final point I want to make about therapist self-disclosure is that it is best to share a personal experience where you initially disturbed yourself about an adversity and then used methods to help yourself, which are similar to those that, with your help, the client is considering to use to address their target problem.

8.9   Using a Range of Techniques

While, the SSI-CBT framework allows you to use a range of techniques, I personally find that techniques that I invent on the spot, which are tailor-made for the client, are often the most useful. Of course I cannot predict what they are but my purpose is to create a method that encourages the client to take away something brief, memorable and impactful, that embodies their healthy thinking that can easily be tied to constructive behaviour.

One issue that I do wish to address here is that of mindfulness, as I am often asked about my attitude towards mindfulness and how I use it in my clinical practice. In terms of approaching what can be termed 'problematic' cognition, the field of CBT can be crudely divided into two camps: those who see such cognitions as problematic and need to be modified and those who see the presence of such cognitions as non-problematic, but our attempts to modify them as problematic. In reality, probably most CBT therapists use a mixture of cognitive modification and mindfulness approaches (where the existence of such cognitions are noted and left to stay or go 'as they please') in their practice and I am no exception in this respect.

While I largely employ a cognitive modification approach, I suggest that clients use a mindful approach after they have engaged in a period of cognitive modification or when they are in danger of getting too wrapped up in cognitive restructuring which may lead to rumination. Here I encourage clients to hold these thoughts in mind without acting on them and to act in ways that are in the service of their goals.

I also help clients to see in SSI-CBT that the initial presence of a dysfunctional process is non-problematic. Rather, what determines whether a person experiences their problem is how they respond to this dysfunction. If they try to eliminate or avoid the dysfunctional process, then this will lead to their problem, but if they respond to it in ways learned in SSI-CBT (either to modify it, allow it to be or a combination of these approaches) then they will deal productively with the dysfunctional process so that it does not become a problem for them.

8.10 Helping Clients to Apply Their Learning

In SSI-CBT, helping clients to apply their learning is central to the success of the process. Traditionally, in CBT, homework assignments are negotiated which enable clients to put into practice outside the session what they have learned in the session. Clients' experiences in carrying-out the negotiated assignments are then discussed in the following session. Of course, this traditional way of working is not possible in SSI-CBT. All you can do with your client is to help them to plan a programme of applying what has been learned in the session and identify and deal with any foreseeable obstacles to carrying out that programme. In addition, in SSI-CBT, it is important, if you can, to help the client to apply their learning in the session. Examples of such in-session work could include appropriate role play, two-chair work, externalisation of voices and imagery.

However, it is often only possible to replicate the adversity that the client finds problematic in imagery. Thus, with the client who is anxious about her mind going blank while giving a speech, you can have her give a brief speech to you in the session, but you can only prepare her for the eventuality that her mind may go blank in imagery. You can't press a switch and have her mind go blank. Indeed, my experience of the perverse nature of being human is that if you wait for your mind to go blank, it doesn't, while it will go blank when you don't know that it will. It is the unpredictability of this and of other adversities that you need to help clients prepare for and deal with.

8.11 Asking Clients to Summarise

At the end of the face-to-face session, it is important to ask clients to summarise what has been covered in the session, what they have learned and what plan of action they are going to implement. If they have omitted any important information, prompt them. If clients can't provide a summary, you might provide one yourself.

8.11.1 Tying Up Loose Ends

In my view, it is best to end the face-to-face session with no outstanding issues to be dealt with. So I ask my client to raise such issues before we close. I particularly use the following question, 'If, when you get home, you wish you had raised one issue with me that you did not raise or asked me one question that you did not ask, what would that be?' In my experience responses to these issues or questions can be quite short and the advantage of tying up such loose ends far outweighs the time you may spend on them. I want clients to leave SSI-CBT committed to a plan of action and raring to go and not disappointed that they did not raise an issue or ask a question.

9

Contact 4: Follow-up

While some single-session purists argue that carrying out a follow-up compromises the integrity of SST,[6] my own view is that doing so is important in that it provides useful information on therapy outcome and service delivery. In Table 9.1, I present a protocol that I use in conducting a follow-up session which in my practice takes place about three months after the face-to-face session has taken place, although the actual interval between the two points of contact may vary.

Table 9.1   Follow-up telephone protocol in SSI-CBT

1.	Check that the client has the time to talk now (i.e. approximately 20-30 minutes)? Are they able and willing to talk freely, privately and in confidence?
2.	Read the client their original statement of the problem, issue, obstacle or complaint. Ask: 'Do you recall that?' 'Is that accurate?'
3.	Would you say that the issue (re-state as described by the client) is about the same or has changed? If changed, list it on a five-point scale as follows:

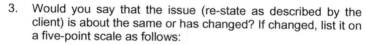

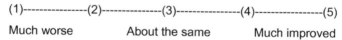

4.	What do you think made the change (for better or worse) possible. If conditions are the same, ask 'What makes it stay the same?'

---

[6] Such writers argue that single session therapy is just that: one single session of therapy (e.g. Hymmen, Stalker and Cait, 2013).

5. Have people around you given you the feedback that you have changed? If so, how do they think you have changed?

6. Besides the specific issue of.... [*state the problem*], have there been other areas that have changed (for better or worse). If so what?

7. Now please let me ask you a few questions about the therapy that you received. What do you recall from that session?

8. What do you recall that was particularly helpful or unhelpful?

9. Have you been able to make use of the session recording and/or transcript? If so, how?

10. How satisfied are you with the therapy that you received? Use a five-point scale as follows:

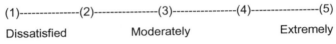

(1)---------------(2)----------------(3)---------------(4)----------------(5)

Dissatisfied   Moderately   Extremely

11. Did you find the single-session therapy package to be sufficient? If not, would you wish to resume therapy? Would you wish to change therapist?

12. Do you have any recommendations for improvement in the service that you received?

13. Is there anything else I have not specifically asked you that you would like me to know?

Thank the client for their time and participation. Remind them that they can contact you again if they require additional services.

9.1   Clients Are More Important than the Framework

I want to end Part I with an important point that is easy to overlook, especially when one is learning SSI-CBT and feels enthusiastic about it. Clients are more important than approaches. As described above, SSI-CBT is a four-contact approach, which, according to Talmon's (1990) definition of single-session therapy, is a cognitive-behavioural approach to this mode of therapy. When people are training in this approach, they are keen for nominated clients to keep to the framework. However, it is important to remember that client welfare is much more important than the integrity of SSI-CBT and therefore if clients need additional sessions it is important to offer them these sessions even though you originally contracted to work within the SSI-CBT framework.

Having said that, I have noticed, somewhat paradoxically, that if I am open to offering SSI-CBT clients more sessions, the less likely they are to want to accept such additional help. But, if I pressurise both myself and my client by believing that once I have offered SSI-CBT it has got to be SSI-CBT, then both of us will become anxious and this is not the best climate for clients to get the most out of this approach to single-session therapy. So the best frame of mind to be in to practise SSI-CBT is a flexible frame of mind, which is precisely the state of mind clients need to access in order to get the most out of the process. Thus, the best way of encouraging flexibility in your clients is first to encourage flexibility in yourself!

PART II

VERY BRIEF COGNITIVE-BEHAVIOURAL COACHING (VBCBC)

Overview

In this second part of the book, I describe an approach to coaching that I have devised entitled 'Very Brief Cognitive-Behavioural Coaching' (VBCBC). I discuss the basic assumptions of this approach; how it can be understood from the perspective of working alliance theory; recommendations concerning when it can be used and when not; and what skills and characteristics both coaches and coaches need to bring to the VBCBC process to enhance its effectiveness. I then concentrate on discussing a process view of this very brief approach to coaching.

10

Introduction to VBCBC

Before I outline and discuss a very brief approach to cognitive-behavioural coaching that I have devised, let me make clear where I stand on a number of topics related to coaching. This will help you understand better this approach, which I have called 'Very Brief Cognitive-Behavioural Coaching' or VBCBC.

10.1 Coaching Is Primarily for Issues of Development

In a book that I wrote recently on the distinctive features of REBT (Dryden, 2015), I pointed out that this approach to CBT distinguishes between therapeutic work that is focused on client disturbance, client dissatisfaction and client development. When a client is disturbed, it is usually about some type of adversity. The goal of therapeutic work with adversity-related disturbance is to help the person deal with the adversity in more productive ways, emotionally, behaviourally and cognitively.

REBT distinguishes between unhealthy negative emotions and healthy negative emotions. The former represents the affective side of psychological disturbance while the latter represents the affective side of dissatisfaction, which is free from such disturbance. Thus, when an adversity exists it is healthy to feel bad but be undisturbed about it and as I have just mentioned REBT calls this state: dissatisfaction. The goal of therapeutic work with adversity-related dissatisfaction is to help the person change the adversity if it can be changed or to adjust constructively to the adversity if it can't be changed and then to move on with their life. Once the person has been helped to deal with their issues of disturbance and dissatisfaction (preferably in that order), they are ready to focus on issues of development or personal growth. The development or growth arena is the one with which coaching is primarily concerned.

I see coaching, therefore, as a way of working with people whose lives are basically OK, which is designed to help them get more out of themselves, their work, their relationships and all relevant aspects of their lives. So far so good and this is a neat and tidy way of dividing up the field. However, people's lives don't fit so neatly into these discrete categories.

10.2 When Adversities Happen During Coaching

Although a coachee might start coaching free from the distraction of dealing with one of life's adversities, it may well happen that they may encounter one during the coaching process. Here are two common examples of this occurring.

10.2.1 An Example of an Adversity Encountered that *Is* Related to the Pursuit of Development-based objectives

First, let me consider a situation where a person experiences an adversity that *is* directly related to their pursuit of a development-based objective. Jane has sought coaching because in order to excel in her chosen career she needs to become an accomplished public speaker and she currently rates herself as average at public speaking. Her coach helps her to set the goal of increasing her competence and confidence about speaking in public and she arranges to give a few talks to kick-start this process. During the first talk, Jane's mind went blank, which she found very difficult to deal with and responded to by running out of the room. She then cancelled her next talk because she had now become anxious in case her mind goes blank again. In this scenario, it is clear that Jane cannot proceed to work towards meeting her development-based objective because she is disturbed about the adversity of her mind going blank and she needs help to deal with this adversity before she can resume her pursuit of her development-based objective.

10.2.2 An Example of an Adversity Encountered that *Is Not* Related to the Pursuit of Development-based objectives

Second, let me consider a situation where a person experiences an adversity that *is not* directly related to their pursuit of a development-based objective. In this second scenario, Jane has again set becoming more confident and competent as a public speaker as her development-based objective and has arranged to give a few talks. During this process, her sister develops an illness which Jane is very worried about. Can Jane compartmentalise her worry so that it does not impact on her coaching work or will this worry preoccupy her to the extent that she can't focus on her development-based objective? If Jane can compartmentalise the worry, coaching can proceed, but if not she needs to be helped to address this worry so that she can resume work towards her development-based objective.

10.2.3 The Skills Question

When considering the issue of coaches helping their coachees to deal with disturbance about adversities encountered during the coaching process and also helping them to deal with dissatisfaction about these adversities so that they can focus fully on their development-based objectives, the question of the skills of the coach becomes salient. In our example, does Jane's coach have these skills? The answer to this question depends on the prior training of the coach. In my view, those coaches who have been originally trained in cognitive behaviour therapy do have the skills to do this, while those coaches who have not been trained in CBT may well struggle in this area and may have to refer their coachees who experience disturbance during the coaching process to cognitive-behavioural coaches who have been trained to deal with disturbance and related dissatisfaction. Once these latter coaches have completed their work with these coachees they can refer them back to the original coaches.

Having dealt with such preliminary issues, I will now discuss 'Very Brief Cognitive-Behavioural Coaching' henceforth referred to as VBCBC. I will:

- briefly describe the approach and will then show how VBCBC can be understood more fully by using the working alliance framework introduced by Bordin (1979) and expanded by me (Dryden, 2006, 2011a);

- present some of the basic assumptions that underpin the approach;

- consider when it can and cannot be used;

- outline some of the skills and characteristics that both coaches and coachees should ideally have that would be helpful to the VBCBC process;

- present the seven stages of the VBCBC process.

11

What is Very Brief Cognitive-Behavioural Coaching (VBCBC)?

What is the nature of VBCBC? In this chapter, I will first describe this approach in a nutshell before using working alliance theory (Bordin, 1979) to put flesh on these bones.

11.1 VBCBC in a Nutshell

Very brief cognitive-behavioural coaching is coaching that is carried out between one and three sessions. If more than one session is contracted then the spacing of the remaining sessions is decided jointly between coach and coachee. VBCBC is designed to help coachees identify development-based objectives, discuss and select ways to achieve these objectives and, if necessary, deal with obstacles that they experience or anticipate that they may experience while pursuing these objectives within this specified time frame. Such obstacles are normally encountered when coachees have a problem dealing with adversities that arise in their lives that may either be (a) directly related to their coaching obstacles (in Jane's case her anxiety about her mind going blank while giving a presentation) or (b) not related to these objectives at all, but which serve to interfere significantly with coaching (in Jane's case her worry about her sister's illness).

11.2 VBCBC and the Working Alliance (WA)

While cognitive-behavioural coaching is normally an ongoing process, both it and the very brief version of it presented here can be understood by considering it from the perspective of working alliance (WA) theory initially introduced by Bordin (1979) and developed by me a number of years later (Dryden, 2006, 2011a). I will focus my discussion here on how WA theory can help illuminate VBCBC. The working alliance between coach and coachee has four domains: bonds, views, goals and tasks.

11.2.1 WA Domain 1: Bonds

A coaching bond refers to the interpersonal connectedness between coach and coachee. This points to, amongst others, (1) the coachee's experience of the coach as offering the core therapeutic conditions (empathy, unconditional positive regard and genuineness) made famous by Rogers (1957), (2) the interpersonal style that the two develop over time and (3) the influence base of the coach (expertise and likeability are two such bases). In VBCBC, coaches have to have the skills to develop an immediate working rapport with their coachees, utilise authentically different interpersonal styles that will facilitate coachee learning and use different influence bases to make a greater impact with different coachees.

11.2.2 WA Domain 2: Views

Views refer to the shared cognitive understandings that coaches and coachees have of the work that they propose to engage in and related issues (e.g. frequency of meetings, fees, confidentiality). It is these views that form the basis of the informed consent that coachees give for the work to proceed. In VBCBC, coaches and coachees need to agree; (a) that they will form a *coaching* contract (as opposed to a *therapy* contract), (b) that this work will be time limited (between one and three sessions), (c) that the coaches' fee is acceptable to their coachees and (d) what the nature of the confidentiality of the work is.

11.2.3 WA Domain 3: Goals

All forms of help are purposive and the objectives of coaching are normally focused on helping coachees to get more out of their personal life, work life and/or their relationships. The main task of coaches here in VBCBC is to help their coachees set objectives that are realistic given the very brief nature of the work. Thus, coaches should ideally help their coachees set one specific coaching-related objective and to encourage coachees to keep this objective in mind throughout the process. I call this objective a 'development-based' objective to make clear that the coach is working with the coachee to further the latter's development or growth.

11.2.4 WA Domain 4: Tasks

Extrapolating from Bordin's (1979) points about the task domain of the working alliance, both coaches and coachee have tasks to carry out in coaching and the focus here is for coaches to help their coachees select ways of achieving development-based objectives that make sense to the coachees and which they can execute in their own life. In addition, coaches need to help their coachees identify and problem-solve any obstacles to achieving the objectives. With respect to the tasks of coaches, from the perspective of WA theory, coaches need to help ensure that coaches see the relationship between their tasks and their development-based objectives in the objective pursuing phase of VBCBC and their tasks and addressing their disturbance in the obstacle addressing phase of the work. In addition, coaches need to ensure that their coachees have the skills to carry out their tasks. Given the time-limited nature of the work there is probably only time to teach coachees new skills that can quickly be learned.

12

Some Basic Assumptions

Very brief cognitive-behavioural coaching is based on a number of assumptions that I will now discuss.

12.1 Coaching Occurs Over the Person's Life Cycle: It's Not a One-Shot Deal

VBCBC concurs with the idea that it can be just as productive for people to seek coaching for short periods of time across the life cycle than it is for them to have one extended period of coaching. Thus, at critical junctures of the life cycle, people may seek coaching assistance designed to help them get the most out of a life transition. When this happens they often won't need to have ongoing coaching, but coaching based on focused very brief interventions such as provided by VBCBC.

12.2 Coaching Starts Before the First Contact and Will Continue Long After the Final Contact

It is tempting for coaches to think that coaching only occurs in formally arranged coaching sessions. However, coaches who practise VBCBC recognise that coachees may well have sought informal coaching help before coming for formal coaching and will continue to seek such informal help after coaching has formally ended. VBCBC coaches take advantage of this fact and seek to utilise the resources available to coachees (personal, interpersonal and environmental) in this approach to coaching rather than just focusing on what they can offer them.

12.3 Build on What's There, Don't Start from Scratch

Following on from the above, VBCBC seeks to makes use of what coachees are already doing that could aid the coaching process. They do not believe that it is important to clear the decks and start from scratch.

12.4 You Do Not Have to Rush

While VBCBC is, by definition, time-limited, this does not mean that coaches have to rush. Effective VBCBC coaches are task-focused but create an unhurried atmosphere while doing so. Here I often use the example of Mesut Özil, the Arsenal midfielder, who no matter what situation he is in on the pitch, always seems to create time and space for himself. In supervising VBCBC coaches, I often encourage them to 'do an Özil' when they appear under time pressure.

12.5 Less Is Often More in VBCBC

When coaches first learn about VBCBC they think that given the time-limited nature of the approach they have to pack in as much as they can into the time that they do spend with coachees. This would be a mistake since the danger here is that such coaches will overload their coachees who may well go away with nothing as a result. Rather, it is often better to help coachees to take away one thing that they can use to get the most out of the area of life on which they have chosen to focus than it is to overload them with many points (Keller and Papasan, 2012). To quote the ancient Greek poet Archilocus: 'The fox knows many things, but the hedgehog knows one big thing.' Thus, VBCBC could also be known as 'Very Brief Coaching for Hedgehogs'.

12.6 Expect Change

It is well known in education that teachers who have high expectations of their pupils get more from them than do teachers with lower expectations (Rosenthal and Jacobson, 1968). This finding is relevant for coaching as well, as coaches who expect more from their coachees, even in a time-limited approach such as VBCBC, will tend to help them more than will coaches who think that little can be done in such a short period of time.

12.7 Human Beings Have the Capability to Help Themselves Quickly under Specific Circumstances

When I have presented VBCBC to coaches, I often hear the comment that there is insufficient time to coach people 'properly' in this very brief approach. This may be the case, but not in all respects, and VBCBC is based on the assumption that under certain circumstances people can respond to a very brief intervention and help themselves in a short period of time. It is partly for this group of people that I devised VBCBC. I will discuss the indications for VBCBC in Chapter 13.

12.8 Coaching Is a Fusion of What Both Parties Bring to the Process

While VBCBC is largely based on the cognitive-behavioural approach to coaching (Neenan and Palmer, 2012), it also takes seriously the pluralistic point that, at times, it is important to privilege coachees' viewpoints during the process (Cooper and McLeod, 2011). Thus, VBCBC is a fusion of what *both* the coach *and* the coachee bring to the coaching process, rather than being a top-down coach led activity or a bottom-up coachee led endeavour.

12.9 It is Important to Draw Upon a Range of Coachee Variables in VBCBC

Given that VBCBC utilises what coachees bring to the process, then it is important for coaches to understand what these variables are. I will discuss this issue in greater depth when I outline the process of VBCBC in Chapter 16.

13

Why Very Brief Cognitive-Behavioural Coaching ... and Why Not

If coaching is usually an ongoing process why should VBCBC be considered given its time-limited nature? In my experience there are a number of reasons for considering VBCBC.

13.1 Indications for VBCBC

There are two sets of reasons for considering VBCBC. The first concerns positive indications and the second concerns pragmatic reasons for this approach to very brief coaching.

13.1.1 Positive Indications for VBCBC

In my view there are two positive indications for VBCBC, one relates to setting up and launching the coaching process and the other relates to dealing with actual or anticipated obstacles to achieving development-based objectives.

13.1.1.1 *Coaching for Autonomous Coachees*

VBCBC is particularly indicated for coachees who are autonomously organised in their personality and prefer to help themselves rather than being helped. When they seek coaching it is to initiate or 'kick-start' a process which they will then take charge of themselves. This fits very well with the aims of VBCBC.

13.1.1.2 *Dealing with Obstacles: Actual or Anticipated*

Coaching, like the course of true love, often does not run very smoothly and coachees may encounter a range of obstacles to the pursuit of development-based objectives, some that relate to the coaching process itself and others that do not (see the case of Jane that I discussed earlier in Part 2). When such obstacles can be dealt with in a short period of time (i.e. 1–3 sessions) by coaches who have the skills to do so, then VBCBC is indicated. Here are two commonly encountered scenarios.

In the first scenario, *coaching has come to an end* and an unanticipated obstacle to the autonomous pursuit of a development-based objective is then encountered by the coachee. In such cases, (a) the original coach may not be available to see the coachee; (b) the original coach may not have the skills to deal with these obstacles or (c) the coachee specifically wishes to consult a cognitive-behavioural coach skilled in doing so, but briefly. VBCBC can help the person deal with the obstacle and they can then resume their autonomous pursuit of their development-based objective.

In the second scenario, an obstacle may be encountered or is anticipated *in ongoing coaching*. If the coach does have the skills to deal with these, then there is no problem. However, if the coach does not have the skills to deal with these, they may refer the coachee to a coach who does have the skills for obstacles-focused VBCBC and once this work has been done the coachee returns to the original coach.

13.1.2 Pragmatic Reasons for VBCBC

In addition to the positive indications for VBCBC discussed above, there are a number of pragmatic reasons why VBCBC should be actively considered.

13.1.2.1 *Cost*

Coaching can be quite expensive and, while potential coachees may get more out of the process if it were extended, they may not be able to afford such ongoing work if they are paying for coaching themselves and have a small personal budget. In this case VBCBC should be offered as it may be within the person's budget.

13.1.2.2 *Limited Organisational Resources*

When an organisation is funding coaching for their employees, the resources available for this activity may be limited. If the resources do not stretch to cover everybody who wants ongoing coaching then limits may be imposed on the number of coaching sessions that will be permitted to enable everybody seeking it to have at least some coaching. In this circumstance, VBCBC can be considered.

13.1.2.3 *Time*

Some people may be able to afford ongoing coaching but may not be prepared to invest the requisite time to it and thus VBCBC may be appropriate given its time-limited nature.

13.1.2.4 *Geography*

Some people who seek coaching may live in remote areas that make travelling regularly for ongoing face-to-face coaching difficult or even impossible. While Skype coaching sessions may be a solution for some, for others who only want face-to-face coaching, VBCBC may be indicated given that it does not ask for a commitment to regular sessions necessitating regular long-distance travel.

13.1.2.5 *Coachees from 'Out-of-town'*

Occasionally I have had requests from people who are visiting London from overseas who wish to see me for coaching for a limited period (most frequently between one or two weeks) when they are 'in town'. VBCBC is indicated for such people.

13.1.2.6 *Coachees Wanting a Taste of Coaching*

Some prospective coachees are interested in ongoing coaching but want to try it first before committing themselves to 'signing up'. In this case, VBCBC provides such a taste and while most coachees then do go on to commit themselves to ongoing coaching because they understand better what coaching entails, occasionally it transpires that a coachee achieves what they were looking for and exit the process at this point satisfied with the outcome.

13.2 Contraindications for VBCBC

Having just outlined the positive indications for VBCBC and the pragmatic reasons why it should be considered, let me deal with some of the contraindications for this approach.

13.2.1 Coachees Who *Require* Ongoing Coaching

When it is clear that a coachee wants coaching in a number of areas of their life where they doing OK, but sense that they could get a lot more from these areas, then they probably require more extended, ongoing coaching and thus VBCBC is not indicated.

13.2.2 Coachees Who *Seek* Ongoing Coaching

Particularly when they are being sponsored, but also when they are self-payers, a number of people actually seek ongoing coaching and would not accept VBCBC if offered. Unless there is a particularly good reason to offer VBCBC, in which case the rationale should be made clear, then these prospective coachees' coaching preferences should be met.

13.2.3 When Obstacles to the Coaching Process Require More Time than VBCBC Can Provide

I mentioned earlier in Part 2 that VBCBC can be offered if coachees encounter obstacles to pursuing their development-based objectives or think that they might encounter such obstacles. Assuming that coaches have the skills to deal with the obstacles, VBCBC is indicated if the obstacle can be dealt with within the three-session maximum paradigm of this approach, However, if coaches judge that more time is needed to deal with the obstacle or if coachees experience several such obstacles then VBCBC is not indicated.

13.2.4 Coachees Who Find It Difficult to Focus and/or Be Specific

As I will discuss presently, effective VBCBC depends, in part, on coaches and coachees being able to focus on development-based objectives and keep to this focus. It is also important that coachees are able to be specific in articulating their development-based objectives and the obstacles that they experience or anticipate experiencing to the pursuit of these objectives. Coachees who have difficulty in focusing and being specific may not be good candidates for VBCBC, especially if they can't demonstrate these having been encouraged by their coaches to do so.

14

Coach Skills and Characteristics that Are Helpful for VBCBC

VBCBC is a form of coaching that is quite demanding on both coaches and coachees. Given this, let me outline in this chapter the coach skills and characteristics that aid the process and increase the chances that the process will be effective. The more of these coaches demonstrate, the more effective the process is likely to be for their coachees. Thus, effective VBCBC coaches do the following.

14.1 Demonstrate the Core Therapeutic Conditions

Perhaps the most seminal article that has been written in the field of counselling and psychotherapy is highly relevant for coaching in general and for VBCBC in particular. Extrapolating from that article (Rogers, 1957) we can argue that change in coaching is enhanced when coachees experience their coaches to be empathic, respectful and genuine. Skilful VBCBC coaches quickly develop rapport with their coaches in a manner that maximises the chances that this happens. One skill that I want to mention here, because it tends to be underrated, is the importance of coaches, whenever practicable, explaining to their coaches what they plan to do in VBCBC and seeking their coachees' permission to proceed. These skills, in my view, operationalise Rogers' conditions of respect and genuineness and form an important foundation for the ethical principle of informed consent.

14.2 Have Realistic Expectations of VBCBC

I mentioned earlier the importance of VBCBC coaches having high, but realistic expectations of what coachees can potentially achieve from a brief coaching intervention. The same is also the case when it comes to what VBCBC has the potential to offer coachees. It is thus helpful for coaches to have realistic expectations from VBCBC and to recognise that it can help to kick-start a coaching process that coachees can then take responsibility for continuing and it can help coachees deal with actual and/or anticipated obstacles to the coaching process in a focused way. To expect more or less of the process is not a helpful coach characteristic.

14.3 Be Active and Directive, but in a Collaborative Way

Most forms of cognitive-behavioural work call upon the helper to adopt an active-directive interactional style and VBCBC is no exception to this principle. It is particularly helpful to the VBCBC process if coaches can adopt this style while, at the same time (a) encouraging activity in their coaches, (b) fostering collaboration with them and (c) preserving their autonomy.

14.4 Use Questions Effectively

It is generally recognised that the use of questions is a powerful tool in coaching (e.g. Stanier, 2016). Therapists and counsellors who were initially trained to refrain from asking questions find the transition to making liberal use of questions in coaching particularly difficult. If such helpers are to become effective VBCBC coaches then they need to deal with their internal barriers to asking questions and learn the following skills: (a) asking questions in a succinct manner, (b) giving coaches time to answer the questions, (c) listening carefully to the answers given in order to determine whether or not their questions have been answered and (d) asking follow-up questions depending on the answers given to the previous question.

14.5 Work Well with an Agreed Focus without Having a Full Understanding of Coachees

Coaches who like to work with the whole person and who prefer to have a full understanding of the person that they will be coaching tend to struggle with the focused discipline of VBCBC. However, it is a helpful skill for coaches to be able to work with an agreed focus and not be daunted by lack of knowledge of coachees. It also helps if VBCBC coaches are excited by the challenge of working under such levels of not knowing.

14.6 Maintain the Agreed Focus

Having negotiated an agreed focus with their coachees, it is a helpful skill for VBCBC coaches to be able to keep to this focus and not to have a problem in interrupting with tact coachees who move away from the focus. Explaining, in advance, the purpose of such interruptions while obtaining permission to do so is also a helpful coach skill.

14.7 Help Coachees to Specify a Meaningful Development-based Objective

It is very helpful if coaches can help their coachees specify a meaningful development-based objective, one that they really want to achieve rather than think they ought to achieve. To be able to do this quickly is also important. Since objectives are more likely to be pursued if they are underpinned by (a) key coachee values, (b) a sense that such objectives have meaning for the person and (c) contribute to the sense that they are leading a life that matters. It is also helpful for coaches to be comfortable working with such existential issues and be able to link them with coachees' objectives.

14.8 Identify and, at Salient Points, Utilise Coachees' Resources and Relevant Experiences

I mentioned briefly earlier that coachees are not blank slates and bring to the VBCBC process a number of resources and relevant experiences that aid this process. It is helpful for coaches to identify and make use of such resources and relevant experiences at particular points in VBCBC.

14.9 Think and Intervene Quickly without Rushing Coachees

It is a helpful skill for VBCBC coaches to be able to do things quickly without rushing their coachees. Thus, they need to be able to think quickly on their feet, develop rapport immediately with their coachees and intervene speedily and efficiently. While being mindful of time, it is also helpful if they are equally mindful of how their coachees process information and are able to moderate their rate of working to ensure that coachees are fully involved in the learning process.

14.10 Communicate Clearly and Seek Feedback

It is particularly helpful if VBCBC coaches are able to communicate clearly and effectively and that they seek feedback from their coachees concerning their level of clarity. When it is apparent that they are not being clear and/or understood, it is helpful for coaches to modify their style of communicating. Thus, being able to implement feedback after seeking it is very important.

14.11 Use Metaphors, Aphorisms, Stories and Imagery

Given the time-limited nature of VBCBC, it is helpful to the process if coaches can employ metaphors, aphorisms and stories and are able to tailor them to individual coaches with humour when appropriate.

14.12 Be Flexible and Have a Pluralistic Outlook

Although VBCBC is a very brief way of working with coachees that is based on cognitive-behavioural coaching (Neenan and Palmer, 2012), it is a framework that calls upon coaches to be flexible in three main respects and it is helpful if coaches can show such flexibility.

First, VBCBC is broad enough to enable cognitive-behavioural coaches to use different CBC approaches in practice. Thus, while it can accommodate CBC practitioners who favour a modification approach to troublesome cognitions and emotions, and those who favour an accepting, mindful approach to such processes, it is particularly attractive to those who consider that there is merit in both these ways of working and can make use of both at different times.

Second, VBCBC welcomes coaches who enjoy casting their practice net widely over the panoply of existing coaching methods and favour using, at times, methods that have their origins outside CBC, even though the purpose of doing so is probably consistent with CBC theory rather than with the theory that originated the technique. As an example, I use transformational chairwork (Kellogg, 2015) to help coaches to change their attitude about an adversity, but don't subscribe to the underlying theory that originally spawned this method. Thus, it is helpful for coaches to have that broad technical perspective.

Third, it is a helpful characteristic for VBCBC coaches to be pluralistic in outlook and (a) have a *both/and* view of working with coachees rather than an *either/or* view and (b) take seriously their coachees' views concerning how best the latter can be coached given the very brief amount of time at their joint disposal.

14.13 Move with Relative Ease from the Specific to the General and Back Again

While VBCBC does call upon both coaches and coachees to focus on a particular life domain of the latter and to specify development-based objectives and actual and/or anticipated obstacles to achieving these objectives, it is helpful if coaches can move with relative ease from the specific to the general and back again. While the main goal of VBCBC is to kick-start the coaching process in one life domain and to deal with any relevant obstacles while doing so, it is helpful if coaches can take advantage of opportunities both to help coachees to generalise learning and also to use general principles and help them to find ways to apply these principles in specific situations.

14.14 View Coaching within the Overall Context of Their Coachees' Lives and Encourage Coachees to Make Use of a Wide Range of Resources

Coaching is best viewed contextually. This means a number of things of which I will mention two. First, it means that the selection of development-based objectives needs to be considered not only from the perspective of how it might enhance coachees' lives, but whether or not coachee can integrate these objectives into their lives. Second, it means helping coachees to see that they have at their disposal a wealth of potential resources that they can potentially make use of when working towards their development-based objectives. It is helpful for coaches to be mindful of these two points during the VBCBC process.

14.15 Help Coachees Identify and Work with Key Obstacles to Pursue Their Development-based Objectives

Because of its triple 'O' focus – *objective, operationalise* (i.e. devising a plan to reach development-based objectives and putting this plan into practice) and *obstacle* – VBCBC does require coaches to be skilled at helping coachees to set objectives, plan to meet them and overcome emotionally based obstacles to achieving these objectives. Earlier in Part 2, I discussed the case of Jane who sought coaching to become a more accomplished public speaker, but was anxious about her mind going blank. It is particularly helpful if coaches have the skills to assist people like Jane to address their emotionally-based obstacles (in Jane's case, anxiety) and to do so quickly so that they can resume a development-based objective focus. In this respect, it is also important to set goals with respect to dealing constructively with the adversity that features in the obstacle.

14.16 Identify and Respond to Coachees' Doubts, Reservations and Objections to Any Aspect of the VBCBC Process

Because of the time-limited nature of VBCBC, it is important that coaches help coachees to commit themselves fully to their development-based objectives, to their action plans and to the activities that comprise these plans. However, as mentioned above, it is possible that coachees will experience obstacles to the VBCBC process which their coaches need to be able to identify and help them address. Coachees may experience doubts, reservations and objections (DROs) to any aspect of the VBCBC process including: their own objectives, action plans and associated activities, the methods that their coaches are employing, what they expected to do in the process and any concepts and ideas that their coaches may offer up for their consideration. Given this phenomenon, effective VBCBC coaches ask their coachees for their reactions to the work that they are doing, encourage the expression of any DROs that coachees may have and are sensitive to the possible DROs that coachees may express non-verbally.

Once doubts, reservations and objections have been identified then coaches need to respond to them with sensitivity, but do need to correct any misconceptions that are implicit in the DROs.

14.17 Negotiate and Review 'Homework Tasks' Effectively

When VBCBC goes beyond a single session, it puts coaches into the area where it is important that they negotiate and review suitable homework tasks with their coachees. While I will discuss this issue later with respect to the different stages of VBCBC, I will make a few general comments here.

14.17.1 Negotiating Tasks

When negotiating tasks with coachees it is important for coaches to:

- actually negotiate such tasks rather than unilaterally assign them;
- give themselves sufficient time to negotiate the tasks;
- ensure that the tasks follow on from what has been discussed in the session;

- encourage coachees to be as specific as possible concerning what they will do, when they will do it and how often they will do it;

- identify and problem-solve any likely obstacles to task completion.

14.17.2 Reviewing Tasks

When reviewing tasks with coachees it is important for coaches to:

- review tasks at the beginning of the following session unless there is a good reason not to do so;

- ensure that coachees did the tasks as agreed and explore and, if necessary respond to, any modifications that they made to the tasks;

- assess and respond to failure to initiate or complete tasks;

- identify coachee learning and capitalise on task success by helping coachees to generalise that learning.

14.18 End the Process Suitably

It is an important skill for coaches to end the process of VBCBC in a suitable way. This means that coaches ensure that coachees leave the process knowing what they have covered and learned and what they need to do to achieve their development-based objectives. Coaches encourage coachees at the end to ask any final questions and raise any final concerns so that there are no loose ends when the work has been completed.

15

Coachee Skills and Characteristics that are Helpful for VBCBC

It will be helpful to the VBCBC process if coachees have the following skills and characteristics.

15.1 Be Realistic about What Can Be Achieved in VBCBC

It is very helpful if coachees have realistic expectations of VBCBC, namely that it is meant to help kick-start a process of self-development in one life domain that they can continue on their own and deal with one or two obstacles along the way. Whether coachees have actively sought very brief coaching or whether they have opted to engage in it because it is all that is on offer, it is important that they go into the process with their eyes wide open.

15.2 Be Ready to Engage Fully in the Process

VBCBC is a time-limited focused approach to coaching which is designed to help coachees set meaningful development-based objectives, devise and implement plans of action to achieve these objectives and to deal with obstacles along the way. It is crucial for coachees to play their active part and fully engage in the process. If any ambivalence that coaches have cannot be quickly dealt with, this will limit what they will achieve from the process

15.3 Focus and Be Specific during the Process

VBCBC does require coachees to focus and to specify (1) a development-based objective, (2) plans of action to implement the objective and (3) any obstacles to the process. The more coachees are able to do this, with help from their coachees, the more they will get from the VBCBC process.

15.4 Integrate Development-based Objectives into Their Lives

While being able to nominate at least one development-based objective is the sine qua non of VBCBC for coaches, it is important that coachees select (with help from their coaches) objectives that can be integrated into their lives. If not these development-based objectives will still be desired, but not pursued. Being willing to work with such integration is helpful for the VBCBC process.

15.5 Move Along the Specific-General Continuum in Both Directions

I mentioned earlier that it is important for coaches to be able to move from the specific to the general and back and to help coachees to do this. No matter how good coaches are on this point, if their coachees can only focus on the specific or on the general, then the latter will not get as much from the process than if they can move along the specific–general continuum fairly easily, in both directions, with appropriate help from their coaches, of course.

15.6 Relate to Metaphors, Aphorisms, Stories, Imagery and Humour

Coaching works best when it has an emotional impact on coachees. One of the ways in which coaches do this is by using tailor made metaphors, stories and imagery and when appropriate to use humour while making interventions. None of this will be helpful unless their coachees can relate to this mode of communication and thus it is important for coaches to discover this early in the process. I will discuss this issue more fully later in the book. When both coaches and coachees share a resonance for such communication it is helpful to the coaching process.

15.7 Be Willing to Put into Practice what They Learn Both Within and Outside Coaching Sessions

As with other forms of helping based on cognitive-behavioural principles, the effectiveness of VBCBC is based, in large part, on the extent to which coachees apply what they learn from coaching sessions. This is particularly relevant when it comes to applying such learning outside coaching sessions, but it is also relevant within sessions too and here coaches can use role-play, two chair work and imagery, amongst other methods, to help coachees rehearse learning inside sessions before they apply it outside sessions.

It is particularly helpful, therefore, for coachees to engage in in-session and extra-session tasks to facilitate the achievement of development-based objectives.

15.8 Make Use of a Range of Extra-Coaching Resources

It is easy to forget that coaching sessions occur within the context of coachees' lives and in those lives there are many resources that coachees can use to further their development-based objectives. Thus it is a helpful characteristic for coachees to identify and take advantage of extra-coaching resources to further their progress in whatever life domains they have targeted for development

Chapter 16

The Process of VBCBC

In this final chapter, I discuss the process of VBCBC. In this respect it is useful to view this process as akin to the process of building a house and I will use this analogy throughout my discussion.

16.1 Stage 1: Getting the Fit Right

In my practice, people either contact me by phone or by email. In the latter case, I invite them to phone me at an agreed time. My main purpose in speaking to people myself[7] is to explain what services I offer which are: ongoing CBT, brief CBT (up to 10 sessions), single-session integrated CBT (SSI-CBT), ongoing cognitive-behavioural coaching, very brief cognitive-behavioural coaching (VBCBC) and couples therapy. When someone applies[8] for my help, I outline briefly the nature of each service and for whom it is best suited and then ask the person for their initial thoughts concerning which service best fits their situation. If they nominate VBCBC, I ask them to give me a brief summary why they think that VBCBC is best suited to the help they are seeking and if there is sufficient consistency between

---

[7] I do not employ a receptionist and even if I did, I would prefer to speak with people directly so that I can explain my services in my own way and answer any questions that people may have.
[8] Garvin and Seabury (1997) make a distinction between an applicant for help and a client. The latter is someone who has given informed consent for the help applied for.

what they say and what VBCBC can offer, I outline a way forward, explain what the costs are and if they are in agreement, I make an initial appointment. This stage is akin to selecting and agreeing to purchase a plot of land on which to build a house.

16.2 Stage 2: Laying the Foundations

Once a plot of land has been selected and purchased, the next step in house building is to lay solid foundations. In VBCBC laying the foundations initially involves coaches and coachees agreeing why they are both here and what can be realistically achieved from this approach. The next step is for both parties to prepare themselves for the process. This involves coaches doing two things. First, they collect data on the resources that coachees think they can bring to the process so that they can encourage coachees to use these resources at salient points of the process. Second, they collect data to help them tailor interventions designed to help coachees get the most out of the VBCBC process. Here are some examples of both strategies:

- Identify what coachees regard as their strengths.

- Identify who coachees regard as their role models.

- Identify how coachees learn.

- Identify coachees' principles of healthy living. For example, my mother used to say to me: 'Son, if you don't ask you don't get'. Later, I modified this to: 'If you don't ask you don't get, but asking does not guarantee getting.'

While a coach may not use all this information for when they work with a particular coachee in VBCBC, the important point is that they have this information at their disposal to use when needed.

16.3 Stage 3: Setting the Development-based Objective

Using our house building analogy, setting the development-based objective is akin to devising a vision for the house which shows what the building will ultimately look like. Given the time-limited nature of VBCBC, it is important for the coach–coachee dyad to select a major objective in one domain of the coachee's life (e.g. work, personal life, relationships, spirituality, physical health etc.). However, coaches may also look out for ways of helping coachees to generalise the work that they do to similar objectives in other life domains, but the prime focus in VBCBC is on one objective in one domain of a coachee's life.

16.3.1 The Features of Development-based Objectives

When discussing development-based objectives with coachees, it is important to bear in mind the features of good development-based objectives:

- They have a direction.
- They may not have a final end-point.
- When they have a final end-point, this point has to be maintained. For example, if a coachee wants to improve their level of resilience, this indicates a direction and if an end-point can be specified, it will have to be maintained. The same is true for example with goals that involve improvements in physical fitness or eating.

- Development-based objectives are broad with specific referents. Thus, if a coachee says that they want to be more resilient, then the coach will help them to identify specific markers of resilience.

16.3.2 Conditions that Facilitate the Pursuit of Development-based Objectives

Development-based objectives are more likely to be pursued and coachees are more likely to persist in pursuing them if:

- they are intrinsically important to coachees rather than extrinsically imposed by other people or organisations;
- they are underpinned by values, purpose and meaning that are important to coachees rather than when they do not rest on these variables;
- this pursuit has intrinsic merit to the coachees rather than when it lacks such merit;
- they can be integrated into lives rather than when such integration is not possible; and
- when coachees are prepared to make sacrifices to sustain their pursuit rather than when they are not prepared to do so.

16.4   Stage 4: Devising and Implementing the Action Plan

Devising and implementing an objective-focused coaching plan is akin to the stage of housebuilding where decisions have to be made about how the vision is going to be realised. Often coachees say that they want to get more out of their life in one or more domains, but often do so without thinking through the practicalities of what taking action to achieve this will mean.

During this phase of coaching, then, effective VBCBC coaches need to do the following:

16.4.1 Ensure that Their Coachees Have the Necessary Skills in their Repertoire to Operationalise the Plan

If any new skills need to be taught they need to be taught quickly. Coaches should bear in mind that there is probably insufficient time *both* to do all that is necessary in VBCBC *and* to teach coaches complex new skills.

16.4.2 Ascertain that Coachees are Prepared to Integrate the Coaching Plans into Their Lives[9]

In general, when coachees are easily able to integrate their coaching plans into their existing lives then they will persist much longer at pursuing their development-based objectives than when such integration is problematic. As such, plan integration is an important issue and coaches should help coachees consider the following questions:

- Are you prepared to devote sufficient time to pursuing your development-based objectives and to do this regularly over time?

- Do you have access to what you need in order to pursue your objectives? If not, can you gain such access? For example, if a coachee who wants to improve their physical fitness does not have ready access to a gym,

---

[9] Objective and plan integration are related issues but are not the same.

which is necessary to implement his plan, then they will find it difficult to do so.

- Do you have the support of relevant significant others? If not, what impact does not having such support have on the implementation of your plan over time? How can you address the issue of lack of support? The more coachees have the support of relevant significant others, the more they will persist with their plan. Consequently, VBCBC coaches will encourage coachees to commit themselves to plans which others are prepared to support. However, if coachees do wish to implement plans that others will not support, then their coaches should help them deal with any issues that may come up in the face of that lack of support. As this is a potential obstacle to pursuing development-based objectives, both coach and coachee need to deal with it as such (see Section 16.5: Stage 5).

16.4.3 One-Session VBCBC

VBCBC is a brief approach to coaching that lasts between one and three sessions. Sometimes coachees want to contract for a fixed number of sessions at the outset while others are prepared to go with the flow and see what happens. When one session of VBCBC has been contracted, then it is important for both coaches and coachees to realise that there will be no opportunity for coachees to try out any plan and to report back. Consequently, coachees need to have confidence both that the objectives are worth striving for and that they can put their action plans into practice either independently or with a little help from selected informal helpers.

When no formal agreement has been made concerning the number of sessions it may happen that at the end of the first session, a coachee has identified a development-based objective, devised an action plan and cannot foresee any obstacles to progress the plan towards the selected objective. In this case, the coach and coachee may agree to stop there, with the proviso that the coachee may return for one or two additional sessions if they do encounter obstacles that they can't deal with on their own and if the total number of coaching sessions does not exceed three.

16.4.4 Homework Tasks in Stage 4

If coachees have contracted for two or three coaching sessions or it soon appears that they will need to go on beyond the first session, then it is important for coaches to help them to negotiate tasks that are suitable for the stage of implementing their action plans. While the main purpose of these tasks is to give coachees the experience of implementing their action plans a subsidiary purpose is to discover any obstacles to carrying out the plan. If the latter are discovered, this may mean that the plans may need to be modified or that the obstacles need to be addressed (see Stage 5). It is important for coaches to review such tasks at the beginning of the following session.[10]

16.5 Stage 5: Identifying and Dealing with Obstacles

This stage is akin to the one where obstacles to house construction can be encountered or anticipated and remedial works be undertaken. In coaching it is the stage where CBT-trained coaches who are working in VBCBC feel comfortable

---

[10] See earlier for a review of important coach skills when negotiating and reviewing homework tasks.

and coaches without such training tend to struggle. This is why training in VBCBC for coaches devotes a lot of time to teaching the requisite skills of dealing with emotionally based obstacles which feature an actual or inferred adversity (see Dryden, 2011b, 2011c). Coaches dealing with coachees' obstacles need to be able to do the following:

- Assess obstacles when working with imminent, specific future examples, if possible.

  The reason for this future emphasis is that it is in keeping with the future focus of coaching and it is easier for coachees to implement learning if the settings in which their implementation will occur are the same as those in which the assessment has taken place. Here it is possible for coaches to use any CBC model of assessment. My own preference is to use the ABC framework of Rational Emotive Behaviour Therapy (REBT) (Dryden, 2011b, 2011c).

- Elicit coachees' goals with respect to the adversities featured in the obstacles and keep the focus on these goals during this phase of the work.

- Help coachees to focus on the problematic cognitions that account for the obstacles and deal with these cognitions.

- Encourage coachees to be specific as possible when dealing with obstacles, but look out for and utilise opportunities to help coachees to generalise their learning about how to deal with similar obstacles.

- Ensure that coachees take, at the very least, one meaningful point from the obstacle-dealing process and have a plan to implement this point (Keller and Papasan, 2012).

16.5.1 When Obstacles Have a Clear Emotional Signature and When They Don't

I have found it useful to distinguish between obstacles in the face of adversities that have a clear emotional signature and those that don't.

When the former are encountered, coachees are able to identify clear disturbed emotions such as anxiety, depression, guilt, shame, hurt and the problematic forms of anger, jealousy and envy.

When the latter are encountered the signature is more behavioural in nature. Here coachees report behavioural difficulty in implementing the action plans that they devised with their coach in Stage 4 of the VBCBC process. This difficulty is revealed in problems initiating or maintaining the agreed action plan. While not universally the case, this difficulty suggests the existence of procrastination and other forms of problems with self-discipline. In my experience, the problems that lack an obvious emotional signature require a greater focus on helping coachees develop their tolerance of discomfort than do those that include such a signature.

16.5.2 Homework Tasks in Stage 5

The purpose of homework tasks in this phase of the VBCBC process is to encourage coachees to face the adversities that feature in their obstacles and to practise thinking healthily while facing them. This is so important because, normally, coachees will either have avoided the adversities or faced them but with unhealthy thinking. and as a consequence they have endeavoured to deal with their disturbed responses to these adversities in ways that prove to be unhealthy and which perpetuate the obstacles. In my approach to VBCBC, the ideal homework assignment is where coaches rehearse a flexible and/or non-extreme belief in the face of the adversity while acting constructively and thinking realistically.

16.6 Stage 6: Ending

While VBCBC involves a follow-up scheduled two or three months after the end of the final coaching session, it is important to bring the active part of the process to a fitting end at the close of the final session. This involves coaches doing three things.

16.6.1 Summarising the Process

First, it involves coaches asking their coachees to provide a summary of the work that they have both done in the process. Here coaches will want to prompt their coachees to fill in any gaps in the latter's summaries

16.6.2 Encouraging Coachees to Make an Explicit Commitment to Development-based Objectives and to the Action Plans

Second, it involves coaches encouraging coachees to make an explicit commitment to both their development-based objectives and to the action plans that they have devised to progress their way to the objective. It is also useful to have coachees plan to remake such commitments and to find ways of reminding themselves of the paths that they have chosen to take and why they have chosen to take them.

16.6.3 Tying Up Any Loose Ends

Finally, it involves coaches encouraging coachees to ask any last-minute questions and voice any lingering concerns about the process which should be dealt with briefly, but effectively. This will enable any existing loose ends to be tied up with the result that coachees can go away on a high, full of determination to begin the independent work that they need to do to make the VBCBC process a success.

16.7 Stage 7: Following-up

It is important for coaches to plan for, ideally at the end of the final coaching session, and carry out a follow-up session with their coaches. My own practice is to do this three months after the final session, but different VBCBC coaches have their own ideas about the optimal interval and also coachees' views on this point also need to be taken into account.

There are two main reasons for conducting a follow-up session. First, it provides important data on the outcome of VBCBC.[11] Second, it provides coaches and/or the organisations hosting the coaching process with important information about service delivery. In short, the follow-up session seeks to provide answers to two questions: (1) How well are *you* doing? and (2) How well am *I* and/or are *we* doing?

Table 16.1 provides the protocol that I use when carrying out a follow-up session which is normally conducted by telephone.

---

[11] If a properly conducted outcome study is to be carried out, then pre- and post- forms of measuring client functioning relevant to the coaching process need to be selected and plausible control group interventions need to be devised and implemented.

Table 16.1   Follow-up telephone protocol

1. Check that the coachee has the time to talk now (i.e. approximately 20–30 minutes)? Are they able and willing to talk freely, privately and in confidence?

2. Read to the coachee their original statement of what the status quo was when they first came to see you and what they wanted to achieve from the coaching process. Ask: 'Do you recall that?' 'Is that accurate?'

3. How successful have you been in achieving your objective? Would you say that the status quo as it was then [*restate as described by the coachee*] is about the same or has changed? If changed, list it on a five-point scale as follows:

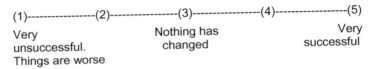

(1)----------------(2)----------------(3)----------------(4)----------------(5)

| Very unsuccessful. Things are worse | Nothing has changed | Very successful |

4. What do you think made the change (for better or worse) possible. If conditions are the same, ask 'What makes it stay the same?'

5. If people around you have given you the feedback that you have changed, how do they think you have changed?

6. Besides the specific issue of … [*state the relevant area*], have there been other areas that have changed (for better or worse). If so what?

7. Now please let me ask you a few questions about the coaching that you received. What do you recall from the sessions that you had?

8. What do you recall that was particularly helpful or unhelpful?

9. If recordings of coaching sessions and/or transcripts of these sessions have been made and sent to coachees, ask: Have you been able to make use of the session recordings and/or transcripts? If so, how?

10. How satisfied are you with the coaching that you received? Use a five-point scale as follows:

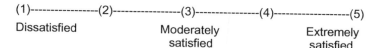

(1)----------------(2)----------------(3)---------------(4)------------------(5)

Dissatisfied   Moderately   Extremely
                       satisfied   satisfied

11. Did you find the coaching package to be sufficient? If not, would you wish to resume coaching? Would you wish to change coach?

12. What recommendations for improvement in the service that you received do you have?

13. Is there anything else I have not specifically asked you that you would like me to know?

Thank the coachee for their time and participation. Remind them that they can contact you again if they require additional services.

16.8 Other Issues

16.8.1 Two Points on Coachee Reflection

It is important for coachees to reflect on the work that they are doing with their coaches and in this respect, I have two points to make.

16.8.1.1 *Preparation and Reflection: Before and After Each Session*

First, I encourage my coachees to get into a reflective state of mind both before attending coaching sessions and after these sessions have finished. Before they attend a coaching session, I encourage them to turn off their mobile phones and tablets and seek a place where they can fully focus on the approaching session and reflect on what they want to get out of it and how they can best prepare themselves for it. I suggest that they do this 30 minutes before the session. In particular, if they have carried out a homework task, I encourage them to focus on what they have learned from the task and how they can capitalise on it as the coaching process unfolds.

After the coaching session has finished, I encourage them to refrain from turning on their phones and tablets for 30 minutes and again seek a place where they can focus fully on what they have learned from the session and how they are going to put this learning into practice. If we have negotiated a homework task, I encourage them to focus on this task and mentally rehearse doing it before they actually do so in reality.

16.8.1.2   *Recordings and transcripts*[12]

The second point that I want to make concerning aiding client reflection arises out of my own idiosyncratic practice of VBCBC. What I do is to record each session and have it transcribed and I send both the recording and the transcript to my coachees so that they can reflect on the sessions that we have had. The feedback that I have received from doing so has been very positive and coachees often say that they have gotten things out of reviewing the sessions that they missed when they having the sessions. Some coachees say that they frequently like to review certain short segments of particular sessions that they have found especially helpful.

---

[12] I pass the cost of the transcripts on to my coachees if they wish to receive copies.

16.9 A Final Word: People are More Important than Approaches

As described, VBCBC is a very brief approach to coaching which lasts between 1 and 3 sessions. But what if coaches need or want more coaching sessions after the final session has been conducted. Unless you are seeing them as part of an outcome study on VBCBC which has very strict criteria on the number of coaching sessions to be undertaken in order for there to be a credible evaluation of this approach, my practice and advice is to offer more sessions on the simple grounds that fostering the integrity of coachees is much more important than preserving the integrity of the VBCB coaching approach! And after all is that not what coaching is primarily about: putting people and their development first?

References

Bordin, E.S. (1979) The generalizability of the psychoanalytic concept of the working alliance. *Psychotherapy: Theory, Research and Practice*, 16: 252–60.

Cooper, M. & McLeod, J. (2011) *Pluralistic Counselling and Psychotherapy*. London: Sage.

Dryden, W. (1997) *Overcoming Shame*. London: Sheldon.

Dryden, W. (2006) *Counselling in a Nutshell*. London: Sage.

Dryden, W. (2011a) *Counselling in a Nutshell*. 2nd edn. London: Sage.

Dryden, W. (2011b) *Dealing with Emotional Problems in Life Coaching*. Hove, East Sussex: Routledge.

Dryden, W. (2011c) *First Steps in Using REBT in Life Coaching*. New York: Albert Ellis Institute.

Dryden, W. (ed.) (2012) *Cognitive Behaviour Therapies*. London: Sage.

Dryden, W. (2015) *Rational Emotive Behaviour Therapy: Distinctive Features*, 2nd edn. Hove, East Sussex: Routledge.

Dryden, W. (2017) *Single Session Integrated Cognitive Behaviour Therapy (SSI-CBT): Distinctive Features*. Abingdon, Oxford: Routledge.

Ellis, A. (1994) *Reason and Emotion in Psychotherapy. Revised and Updated*. New York: Birch Lane Press.

Ellis, A. & Joffe, D. (2002) A study of volunteer clients who experienced live sessions of rational emotive behavior therapy in front of a public audience. *Journal of Rational-Emotive & Cognitive-Behavior Therapy*, 20: 151–8.

Garvin, C.D. & Seabury, B.A. (1997) *Interpersonal Practice in Social Work: Promoting Competence and Social Justice*, 2nd edn. Boston, MA: Allyn & Bacon.

Hayes, S.C. (2004) Acceptance and commitment therapy: Relational frame theory, and the third wave of behavioural and cognitive therapies. *Behavior Therapy*, 35: 639–65.

Hymmen, P., Stalker, C.A. and Cait, C-A. (2013) The case for single-session therapy: Does the empirical evidence support the increased prevalence of this service delivery model? *Journal of Mental Health*, 22: 60–71.

Jones-Smith, E. (2014) *Strengths-based Therapy: Connecting Theory, Practice and Skills*. Thousand Oaks, CA: Sage Publications.

Keller, G. and Papasan, J. (2012) *The One Thing: The Surprisingly Simple Truth behind Extraordinary Results*. Austin, TX: Bard Press.

Kellogg, S. (2015) *Transformational Chairwork: Using Psychotherapeutic Dialogues in Clinical Practice*. Lanham, MD: Rowman & Littlefield.

Lazarus, A.A. (1993). Tailoring the therapeutic relationship, or being an authentic chameleon. *Psychotherapy: Theory, Research, Practice, Training*, 30: 404–7.

Neenan, M. and Palmer, S. (eds) (2012) *Cognitive-behavioural Coaching in Practice: An Evidence Based Approach*. Hove, East Sussex: Routledge.

Ratner, H., George, E. and Iveson, C. (2012) *Solution Focused Brief Therapy: 100 Key Points and Techniques*. Hove, East Sussex: Routledge.

Reinecke, A., Waldenmaier, L., Cooper, M.J. and Harmer, C.J. (2013) Changes in automatic threat processing precede and predict clinical changes with exposure-based cognitive-behavior therapy for panic disorder. *Biological Psychiatry*, 73: 1064–70.

Rogers, C.R. (1957) The necessary and sufficient conditions of therapeutic personality change. *Journal of Consulting Psychology*, 21: 95–103.

Rosenthal, R. and Jacobson, L. (1968) *Pygmalion in the Classroom*. New York: Holt, Rinehart & Winston.

Stanier, M.B. (2016) *The Coaching Habit: Say Less, Ask More and Change the Way You Lead Forever.* Toronto, ON: Box of Crayons Press.

Talmon, M. (1990) *Single Session Therapy: Maximising the Effect of the First (and Often Only) Therapeutic Encounter.* San Francisco: Jossey-Bass.

Zlomke K. and Davis TE., III (2008) One-session treatment of specific phobias: A detailed description and review of treatment efficacy. *Behavior Therapy,* 39: 207–23.

Index

CPSIA information can be obtained
at www.ICGtesting.com
Printed in the USA
BVHW01s0214291117
501448BV00008B/155/P